Money Mindset

Stop Manifesting What You Don't Want and Shift Your Subconscious Mind into Money & Abundance

Law Of Attraction Short Reads, Book 1

By Elena G. Rivers

Copyright Elena G. Rivers © 2020

www.loaforsuccess.com

1

Disclaimer Notice:

Please note the information contained in this
document is for educational and entertainment
purposes only. Every attempt has been made to
provide accurate, up to date, and completely reliable
information. No warranties of any kind are expressed
or implied.

Readers acknowledge that the author is not engaging
in the rendering of legal, financial, health, medical, or
professional advice. By reading this document, the
reader agrees that under no circumstances are we
responsible for any losses, direct or indirect, which are
incurred as a result of the use of the information
contained within this document, including, but not
limited to, errors, omissions, or inaccuracies.

Contents

Ready to Transform Your Money Mindset?

Money doesn't grow on trees!

Who do you think you are?

Don't be so greedy!

Setting money goals is not spiritual!

All rich people are sad and unhealthy...

What's the point of making more money if you have to pay more taxes?

Making more money will take away my time and freedom.

Making money is only for immoral and greedy people...

If you start making more money, you will lose all your friends.

Making money is dangerous...if you get wealthy, everyone will want to steal from you!

Making money is a hassle...who wants that?

The limiting beliefs above are just the tip of the iceberg. And if you picked up this book, chances are, you are already familiar with most of them, if not all of them.

I would even say you are aware and conscious of the fact that these beliefs exist in the minds of so many people. Maybe, they also existed in your mind.

However, since you picked up this book, I would say you want to create more money and abundance into your life.

No matter what stage of your journey you are at, this book will help you. Why? Well, this book is a very simple system. It will give you the tools to dive deep. So that you can make friends with your subconscious mind and become aware of negative patterns that are holding you back from manifesting more money into your life. Whether it's though growing your business, changing your job, or other sources.

My intention for you is to give you the tools for you to experience profound relief and emotional freedom.

There will be no bashing or shaming in this book. Not my goal. Although some parts of this book may come as very honest and direct.

We all carry emotional traumas and negative patterns that are holding us back from reaching the next level in our lives. These patterns usually take over our freedom.

Even wealthy people may still carry some of these negative patterns which explains why some people get stuck at a certain income level. In contrast, others can easily double, triple and quadruple...

No judgment here! For me, personally, my issue was that I would get stuck at the same income level. Even as I was working harder and harder (as a business owner) while investing in my education (self-development, sales, marketing), something would just hold me back or make me sabotage myself.

Some people experience similar blocks that make them manifest what they don't want.

Well, my friends, it's time to unleash freedom, peace, and abundance!

It's safe for you to grow, it's safe for you to make more money, and it's safe for you to achieve your dreams.

Never be ashamed of who you are, and always control your mind!

Unfortunately, as children, we have no idea how to control our minds and what to put in them. Unless you were born into a family of spiritual psychics who also happened to be wealthy entrepreneurs!

Believe it or not, I do have a friend who was born in such a family, and what I share in this book is something normal to him, he knew this as a 7-year-old kid. Really!

But most of us...well...go back to your childhood. What can you see? Maybe mommy and daddy need to talk alone. And you are there on the stairs, curious to see what was going on...

Ready to Transform Your Money Mindset?

The conversations around you...in whispers...are they about prosperity and abundance and how great things were going?

Probably not. Well, at least not in my case. Don't get me wrong, I love my parents, and it's not their fault, they were taught the same negative pattern and program.

I will even say this – some people around me would judge me for writing this book. The book has got the world *money* in the title. Maybe it's a scam or a gimmick, who knows what!

Oh (and my favorite one) how can a woman write a book about money? I mean the money mindset? It's not even how to get more sales, or how to invest kind of book. It's some woo-woo-ish mindset book, and it talks about some unconscious mind BS.

No, I am not promising this book will make you millions overnight. The only thing I can promise is this... Just read it and take notes (I recommend you read it several times). Open your mind to new possibilities! You will be able to get rid of negative patterns that are holding you back from creating the next level of abundance in your life.

Perhaps you already know what to do to make more money, but you just don't do it. For some reason, you procrastinate. Maybe you invested in some expensive business training, and then you quit. Or, perhaps you wanted to ask for a pay rise, and you didn't. Or maybe you were talking to that prospect on the phone, and for some reason, you felt bad for making an offer. Or perhaps you discounted yourself way too much.

Sometimes, money blocks may even manifest in other ways. For example, you feel tired, or you even manifest an illness. It can be your subconscious mind sending signals to your body to make you sick so that you are not able to take action. Because if you do take action, you could make more money and become a different person. And for some reason, your subconscious mind associates money with something terrible, something evil...

One of my female friends wanted to launch her side business for years...yet she always felt stuck and had excuses. She procrastinated and felt bad about it.

After going through the material covered in this booklet, she finally realized what was holding her back. She was afraid that with her business, she would be making more money than her husband and that he would leave her because of that.

The realization came straight out of her subconscious mind, as she was meditating after reading this book.

 (I will show you a very practical way to meditate to help you "cleanse out" all the negative beliefs from your subconscious mind later).

For years, she had no idea, even though she was working with a life coach and a therapist. Everyone thought it was the confidence or motivation issue. Or maybe she had no idea how to market herself.

And she felt too afraid to share her ideas with her husband too, because deep inside she thought it would hurt him, can you believe it!

Poor thing! Luckily it's all good now. What happened is that after shifting her personality (aka her personal reality, as Doctor Joe Dispenza likes to say), she took action to start her side business.

11

Finally, taking action was not a problem, she just felt like doing it. She enjoyed it. Her husband loved the idea, by the way. Eventually, her company took off, and now she runs it together with her husband, who felt very relieved he could change his career. Everyone is happy!

I have witnessed many transformations like the one above. And it's not even about a person making more money. It's about profound transformation and releasing all the negative patterns that are holding you back from living your life to the fullest.

Whatever happened to you, don't worry. Whatever your background is, I believe in you, you can do this.

Maybe you are like me, the first one in your family to take charge of the money mindset so that you can create more abundance into your life...

So amazing! You are breaking old patterns in your family and creating a new path for the new generation...I am so proud of you.

Never feel ashamed for wanting more money and abundance! This book will show you how to "naturally fix" your mindset, changing your story, and becoming a new person. That new person, let's call him or her *The Reader2_0*, will have a totally new self-image.

That new self-image will be aligned to your vision and what you want in life. What is hard for you now is simple, easy, and NORMAL for the Reader 2_0.

Remember...

Prosperity mindset is something very practical that can be learned. Repetition is key here! You also need to allow yourself to keep your mind open. Let go of different judgments...

I know for a fact that you might judge me, this booklet and even yourself.

And it's OK. Don't judge yourself about judging yourself and judging others. And don't fear the fact that you may fear something.

Just move forward with conviction and confidence!

***

Extra Recommendation for You:

To improve your money mindset, you need to know exactly what your blocks are and how you can easily release them.

In order to do so, I highly recommend you take this free Money-Mindset-Vibration test:

www.LOAforSuccess.com/money-test

Now- time to take some meaningful action here to help you transform!

Let's do this!

Thank you for taking an interest in this book. I genuinely believe it has the power to change your life.

Before we dive into the mindset shifts, be sure to read through the next page as I have a free newsletter & surprise gift that I am offering. When combined with the teachings shared in this book, you will be given the advantage that will make everyone around you wonder what it is that you are doing.

See you on the next page!

Ready to Transform Your Money Mindset?

A Special Offer from Elena to Help You Manifest Faster.

The best way to get in touch with me is by joining my free email newsletter.

You can easily do it in a few seconds by visiting our private website at:

www.LOAforsuccess.com/newsletter

The best part? When you sign up, you will instantly receive a free copy of an exclusive LOA Workbook that will help you raise your vibration in 5 days or less:

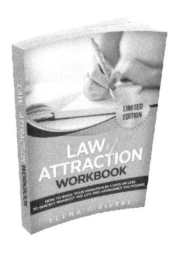

You will also be the first one to learn about my new releases, bonuses, and other valuable resources to help you manifest more money and abundance by shifting your mindset and energy.

Sign up now, and I'll "see you" in the first email.

Love,

Elena

PS. Any problems with your sign up, please email me at:

info@loaforsuccess.com

or reach out to me via my website:

www.LOAforSuccess.com

Chapter 1 What Would it Feel Like to Be More Abundant?

But...If I make more money, then someone will lose it...?

My life will be complicated.

Perhaps I will have to turn into a more responsible person. And what about my friends? What if they assume I am always the one paying for everything, and I will eventually run out of money?

And what if I make a bad investment and lose it all? What if someone decides to go after me and sue me for nothing, just to try and get my money?

What about my family and friends? What if they won't accept me or stop talking to me? And, finally, since I am a spiritual person, I feel like making more money can get me off my spiritual path. I live in 5D now, what if I make more money and I lose my spiritual experiences?

***

Shame. Guilt and Fear.

Our mind loves all three! Unless you have been doing some deep self-development work since you were a kid or your parents taught you how the human mind works, most likely, your thoughts operate around shame, guilt, or fear. I don't know the exact proportion and, since I am not a psychic, I have no idea what is going on in your mind.

I am just good at understanding patterns and how they drive our behaviors.

So, if you lack money, or you can manifest, create, or make more of it, even if you work hard, it's because of fear, shame, or guilt.

The funny part is that we don't know what we don't know. Consciously, we may think we are all good. We are learning. We are growing, we are setting intentions. We are OK. We are already in that small % of people who want to master their mindset. We know that mindset is critical.

So, here's the little game you can start playing with your mind...

We tend to focus on the negative because of fear-based programming. Everything around us is fear-based. Humans will take more action to avoid pain. (so, we are driven by the fear of pain or punishment) rather than to gain more pleasure (in our case, it's money, wealth, abundance, income, whatever you want to call it).

Tony Robbins once said that, in order for us to take action, it has to be either desperation or extreme inspiration (I am paraphrasing his words here, it's not the exact quote, but you know what I mean).

Most of the messages we soaked in, both as children and adults, are fear-based, and we don't even realize it. Until now!

Fear vs. loved based messages is something I am very passionate about. It's something I realized after reading a copy-writing book called *Loved Based Copywriting* by a lady named Michele PW. (actually, it's a whole loved-based series on marketing,

mindset, and copywriting, if you are into t
stuff).

I experienced a very profound spiritual awakening from reading that book. Yes! A spiritual awakening after reading a business/ copywriting / marketing book. Can you imagine?

Some people experience spiritual awakening after taking Ayahuasca or working with some spiritual teacher.

And Elena awakened after reading a copywriting/marketing book! True story! BTW I know a few students of marketing who awakened because of that...studying marketing! Why? Because most of the marketing materials are fear-based. When you realize how it works, you also understand how the World operates, and it awakens you. You want to do something different. You want to do something love-based, something that will work long-term while helping other people (and yourself) without manipulating them and their fears or insecurities. You want to become a conscious creator.

So, here's how it works. Ask yourself about:

-your thoughts (don't judge yourself, just be aware of them)

-your actions and their results – did you take action driven by fear or by love/passion?

-all the marketing messages you see – do they appeal to your fears and insecurities?

-your education and your childhood – what did your parents use to motivate you and educate you? Fear of punishment?

This world is driven by fear. It's one of our basic instincts, after all. Our brain is driven by fear, and it only wants to protect us, to be safe.

Let's go back to the Paleolithic area...to survive, we had to be part of the tribe...And, fear would protect us.

And here we are, in the 21st century...still living in fear, or fearing fear. Or fearing the fact that we are fearing fear and feeling guilty about it.

Unfortunately, most of the time, fear programs us for lack and poverty. And, even if you want to take conscious and meaningful action to shift yourself out of that funk, chances are, your thoughts still align with your fears.

Your mind works like a search engine. So, if you are always thinking about your fears and the worst-case scenarios, your mind will show you even more negative situations. Your mind loves those negative "upsells"!. Take it, here is one more negative scene for you, I know you love this stuff!

Lately, I have been looking into working with a mentor, I heard lots of good things about him. So I googled his company and added "success stories" to it because I was looking for inspiration. I wanted to see how other people transformed using his teachings.

At the same time, one of my friends, who is a bit more skeptical, google his name and added "scam" to it.

Nothing wrong with that, you can google whatever you want. And whatever it is that you focus on- your mind will find the evidence for it.

So, in my case, I found the information that the company and the programs and legit. And I got inspired by people who used those programs and reached out for more information.

However, my friend assumed it was not a legitimate company and forced herself to prove her thoughts right. Once again-nothing wrong with that. In some cases, it's good to be skeptical, and I am not saying that you should always believe everyone and what they say. Do your due diligence.

What I want to draw your attention to is that your mind is like a google search engine.

Let's say you work in sales. Or you are making sales to grow your own business. If in your mind, you assume that you love talking to people, and that you are doing them a big favor by making them offers. You always attract great clients, it's normal for you, and your mind will align you with the evidence and actions that will make your life easier.

However, if your mind goes like:

Oh no… What if I get on the phone with them and in the end, I will share my price and they will tell me it's too much?

And what if we work together and I don't deliver results?

What if they post a negative review about me?

What, if, what if…and only the negative.

So, from now on, whenever you catch yourself in those negative what if's, accept them (don't judge yourself for having them).

Take a piece of paper and write them all down. For example:

What if people don't like my book?

What if they don't like the way I write?

25

Chapter 1 What Would It Feel Like to Be Rich?

What if people think it's too direct and honest?

I am trying to accommodate two different reader avatars...there will be spiritual / law of attraction people, and there will be business owners as well.

What if those spiritual people think I am too salesy and talk too much about money? Maybe they just want me to do cookie cuter books on how to manifest winning the lottery...

(yea, as if it was something that statistically everyone can do and as if it was the ONLY way to make more money).

And those business people, or high-performance people...what if they think I am too woo-woo?

They may see my other books in the law of attraction series. And the series for this book is called Law of Attraction.

OMG...and what if they post a one-star on my book even without reading and purchasing it? Because they don't like the title, or because they got triggered by it?

Did I offend them?

I don't think I should be doing this. I shouldn't be sharing and writing...

Who am I anyway, I am not even a native speaker of English, I had to learn it.

Everyone always laughed at me at school...

Am I safe? What if they laugh at me?

OK...So I am being transparent here, and I am sharing my thought process. I have written it all down. Please, do the same. You know my stuff and my negative thoughts (no worries, I don't need to know yours). Yes, I also have negative thoughts. Some people think that if you do any kind of spirituality work (I have written several books in spirituality), you should always be happy and positive.

One again, I am getting another negative thought – *What if I lose some of my readers? What if they think I am not spiritual enough because I also think negative thoughts?*

Stay calm, Elena. It's ONLY your subconscious mind. We are cleansing and purging!

If your mind always eats fast food, processed food, sugars, and crappy carbs, and out of a sudden, you want to go super clean food plant-based, there will be a detox period. Ad when you are detoxing, it feels weird, it might even feel like you're getting sick.

But it's always worth it!

OK, so I assume you are a good reader and student, and you have already written out your fears and negative thoughts.

If you didn't do your homework yet, you will be grounded (kidding here, I was trying to tease you with some fear-based messaging).

So, right now, we are going against the grain, because in the self-development and spiritual teachings, we are always told to focus on the positive.

And I totally agree!

But before we focus on the positive, it feels so good to get rid of the negative. And it's hard to get rid of it if you are not fully aware of what the negative thoughts in your mind are and what they are trying to protect you from.

So, once again, even though I am all for the positive, I encourage you to write down your current fear-based, negative thoughts.

Now, take another piece of paper and re-write them. Now, it's time to use your mind in a different and much more empowering way...

So, instead of saying:

What if I publish this book and people don't like it?

I ask myself: What if I publish this book and people love it?

Other examples:

What if I call this prospect now and they buy? What would it feel like?

What if I apply for that job, and I get it? What would it feel like?

What if I work less and make more money? What would it feel like?

BTW, you can also use this love-based mindset (aka your mind is a search engine technique) to improve other areas of life.

What if I go on this diet and I love it?

What if I drink those smoothies every day, and my skin looks great?

What if I stop drinking and still have fun while going out?

So, this is the first step. Switch your mindset from fear-based to love-based. Picture the image in your mind and really feel it. Loved-based mindset will connect you with the right ideas, it will guide you. It will propel you to take purposeful and inspired action in alignment with your vision.

Whenever you meditate, focus on your thoughts and let them be. If you catch any negative thoughts trying to get you off track, be sure to re-write them to positive thoughts.

You can google yourself with a "success story" at the end of the search phrase. Or, you can google yourself with "why it didn't work." It's up to you.

And the funny thing is, whatever you focus on, your mind will find the evidence in its search engine...

So, want kind of evidence will you be looking for?

Don't be afraid to dive into the negative, but be sure it's not a habit...If you dive into the negative, it's only to allow negative patterns to come to the surface and then remove them fast by replacing them with positive thoughts and searches.

Afer that, yes, focus on the positive. And it will feel so good, you will feel so free. Try it a few times and let us and other readers know the results by posting a review. We would love to hear about your mindset shifts!

Oh…but, what if I start transforming my mindset and shifting my personality, and people think I am a weirdo?

Yes, those negative, fear-based thoughts appearing once again. Nothing to be ashamed of. I have them as well, and then I use the process I shared with you above to change the direction of my search.

What if people fall in love with who I am becoming, and they get inspired by what I do?

What if more people switch to loved-based, and we transform the world into a happier and more abundant place? And what is the best way to change the world? Can we even change it? Well, my humble opinion is that we should change ourselves. The hardest thing to do!

It's not easy to convince our subconscious minds to change. But, focus on the process, it's already started.

And I am pretty sure that the next months, something will be changing in your life. The law of attraction will be activated because now, you think differently. You use your mind to find solutions, not problems.

Don't be afraid to be different, don't be afraid to be the first one in your family or amongst your friends to actually create incredible financial success. And don't be afraid to be a spiritual or self-development nerd. The world needs more open-minded and loved-based nerds like us!

Guess what, many people will be inspired.

Be very mindful of your time, off and online. Be a nerd, be a weirdo...and if you have a look at what everyone else is doing...in most cases, it's not for you.

Focus on you, and protect your mind. Now you know about the love and fear-based messaging. The fear-based messaging will tell you that you are not good enough, and you can't do it. Get rid of it, get rid of those fear-based weeds, and plant beautiful, love-based flowers of abundance...

Being in that 1% is different. And yes, some people may not like it, because they are in the old programming, the old paradigm. I have some good news for you, though. As you shift your mindset into a more abundant one, you will also attract new people into your life. And those people will understand you, and you will grow together.

Oh, but if all my friends are so successful, I will have to be even more successful!

BOOM, another fear-based thought busted. What if, what if. Fear, fear, fear. But hey, money, and abundance that also aligns with happiness is for people with high standards. High standards are based on love, not fear. So, nothing to be afraid of!

Extra Recommendation for You:

To improve your money mindset, you need to know exactly what your blocks are and how you can easily release them.

In order to do so, I highly recommend you take this free Money-Mindset-Vibration test:

www.LOAforSuccess.com/money-test

Chapter 2 Why Feeling More Positive Is NOT Enough to Manifest More Money

I have said it already. I am all about positivity (as long as the negative weeds are taken out!).

But, I feel like many people think that positive thinking is enough to manifest abundance. Yea, right now, I am writing more for spirituality and law of attraction people! For those of you money and business people - you already know this. However, I will still try hard to entertain you in this chapter at least and make sure you are still getting value from it...

Be intentional about making money. You need to combine your positive thinking with money-making intentions and then -activities. If you still have no idea what steps to take, set the intention for it to be a temporary state. And yes, be positive, visualize and

do the exercises from the last chapter so your mind
can positively activate its search engine.

But, at the same time, take any action to find ideas
that can help you get closer to your money goals.

Positive thoughts are ONLY positive if they translate
to taking positive action. I know a lot of people in the
LOA spiritual community who just think positive, and
nothing happens. And I also know spiritual and LOA
people making a lot of money. Guess what...they
combine attraction with action. All of them create
products (courses, programs, and books) and market
them.

It's not that they just manifest their money out of
nowhere and post online videos for fun. Yes, they
want to help people. But they all operate as
businesses. And to stay in business, they must be
profitable. They need money to pay not only
themselves but also their teams, employees, etc. they
also have to pay taxes. So yea, they are not posting
online content just for fun. It's a part of their
business, and there is nothing wrong with that. In

fact, the world needs more uplifting and positive enterprises and companies that really want to help people.

They are working and taking action...And they manifest! They are adding value and selling that value, and they manifest!

I think it's pretty obvious, and it's not my intention to offend anyone. But sometimes it hurts me. One reader once wrote to me, sharing how she wanted to manifest more money.

I asked her:

OK, so what did you do so far?

Well, she was trying to stay positive (however by the tone of her email I could say she felt nervous), and she kept visualizing, affirming, and taking salt baths.

But she wasn't taking any action at all. What made it worse is that she was very close to being evicted!

Chapter 2 Why Feeling More Positive Is NOT Enough

As someone who is into the law of attraction and spirituality...and all that stuff...meditation, visualization, and affirmation.

Please don't do it to yourself! You also gotta take action! Align your mindset with money-making activities (there is a little bonus at the end of this book, to give you some practical "manifestation" ideas).

In the last chapter, I gave you a simple example of how law of attraction works...

You use your mind to search for ideas, and you take action on them. You work on your reticular activating system...

Or...if you already have an idea, for example, you want to write a book but are too scared of criticism, you can use law of attraction to re-write your story and take action. You can do it in your mind first (exactly as described in the previous chapter) so that you remove the negative blocks holding you back. Then, you can focus on the next practical step. How about writing an outline for your book?

Chapter 2 Why Feeling More Positive Is NOT Enough

I have a friend who is a Life and Law of Attraction Coach, and he had been around the spiritual community for over 2 decades.

He shared with me that he and his team (yes, it is a business!) always freak out when reading people's applications...

This is what he said:

Some people come to us asking for coaching, and they really think they can just visualize and affirm, and everything will happen for them. They usually count on winning the lottery. Then, I ask them, why do you think we can help you?

He always tells them:

Well, I worked hard to create my own company and build my own team. We develop programs that help people, and we sell them.

Yes, we all use the law of attraction as well; we stay positive; we do conscious loved-based marketing.

Chapter 2 Why Feeling More Positive Is NOT Enough

(this is why we don't take money from people we know we can't help, and we don't enroll clients who are not ready for our programs).

We are all into spirituality and self-development.

But our coaching is aimed at people who are already following their passion, taking action, and are looking for that next shift because they feel like something is blocking them from creating more success in their lives.

Lots of people think that if they win the lottery, it will solve all their problems. Here's the thing- wealthy people or people on their way to wealth, don't count on winning the lottery. It's not their only option. They know that there are hundreds, if not thousands of opportunities out there. And your mind can and will lead you towards those opportunities.

And I swear to God...I could publish dozens of books, just copying and pasting emails from people asking me how to manifest winning the lottery.

Chapter 2 Why Feeling More Positive Is NOT Enough

I feel so sorry for such a mindset. Once again, it's a mindset that can be shifted. I am not attacking you or anything!

For example, If I say that smoking is stupid, and you smoke, you will probably get offended. But, I didn't say you are stupid, I said that smoking is stupid. And you can get rid of that. I used to be a smoker myself too.

And yes, I think that the entitlement mindset of "I just want to win the lottery" is not the best mindset you can get, and it is a bit stupid, childish, and immature.

But...once again, if you think it's your only option and you cling to it for some reason, I don't mean to offend you. I hope that this book will connect you with other options.

How do you think LOA gurus manifest their abundance? Did they all win the lottery? I will leave you with this question for now, and we will focus more on LOA gurus and how they manifest abundance in the next chapters.

Chapter 2 Why Feeling More Positive Is NOT Enough

(I will also make you come up with ideas as for how you can do something similar, even if you don't want to be a guru, leader, teacher, businessman, etc.,).

There are many options, I will share everything I know.

***

But now...back to Mindset!

I know...I know...those of you who thought this book will share some secrets or gimmicks to help you win the lottery so that you are all set for life. Perhaps you even think:

But what about those LOA success stories of people who won the lottery?

Yes, it's possible. But once again, I wouldn't count on it as your primary option. The question is – is winning the lottery enough? And are you capable of keeping that money and investing it wisely? Wealthy people (and those on their path to wealth) think differently about money, taxes, tax structure, and all those things that poor souls have no clue about. They are just smarter with their money decisions.

I personally think that, on an energetic level, many wealthy people could actually win the lottery if they tried to. But they just don't do it, because most of them think it's stupid and their minds are focused on other sources of wealth creation, with a much higher level of success.

But, energy and mindset wise, they can be much more aligned to winning the lottery, than a person who is desperate and thinks of the lottery as their only option to create wealth.

Some people are capable of temporarily raising their vibration and manifest winning the lottery, yea, I will give you that.

It's possible. But...most of them are not able to keep that vibration because when they get the money, their old fears and limitations scream "go away money I don't feel secure with you."

Chapter 2 Why Feeling More Positive Is NOT Enough

On a pure skill level, many lottery winners just mismanage their money because once again, they are not used to it.

So, once again, it all comes down to mindset. Most people don't even feel comfortable with 5, 10, or 20 k in their bank account.

Most people are not able to save anything, even if they are making good money in their jobs or businesses. Why is that?

Overspending and mismanaging money is also led by fear. So, you can make it and then you can lose it.

It happened to me and my first super successful business. I reached my higher income goal, but I was all over the place. It felt so intoxicating.

And...my money mindset wasn't there. I wasn't used to making money.

And, so I took self-sabotaging actions, and instead of growing, I began shrinking.

Chapter 2 Why Feeling More Positive Is NOT Enough

Then I felt depressed because I thought I would lose my hard-earned income. And yes, I was losing it, and I ended up in debt. So, what I did then, I was blaming the money itself, and I was blaming some business partners and clients. I was blaming taxes, regulations, and politicians.

I wasn't blaming myself and my mindset.

Then, I felt even more afraid of money. I went into a deep hippie-dippy stage. Money is evil! It's not spiritual, it leads to anxiety and depression.

Finally, I decided to re-build myself...and I got myself back on track. But...on my current journey, I chose to focus on my mindset first. I am doing exactly what I am sharing in this book. This is why it's so practical!

I am shifting my limiting beliefs. And I tell you this – the best way to permanently raise your vibration is to shift from a victim-style mentality to the Responsible Mindset.

Radiate the energy of control and power. No, I don't mean the power over other, less privileged people, and I don't mean manipulation. Not a fan of all that stuff.

The only manipulation I tolerate is – the manipulation you do on yourself and your own mind.

Ethical mindset manipulation.

Positively manipulate your own mindset. Now, you can start shifting into the new reality of abundance.

Yes, those first steps will be a bit painful, and you will feel a bit uncomfortable. But don't give up. Think about a little kid learning how to walk. It keeps trying, it's courageous, even though it keeps falling down all over again. Does it think or say: I guess, walking is not for me, I think I will give up. It's just not for me, I am not passionate about it, I don't have the skillset to learn how to walk. It's too expensive and very time-consuming!

Of course not, the kid will continue walking...growing that walking muscle. Well, changing the way you think, changing your mindset can be a bit painful and challenging at first, but I promise you, it's only painful in the beginning. Everything is painful at the beginning. Any skill. Learning a foreign language is painful at the beginning, what if you forget those new words or say something grammatically incorrect and get laughed at?

Well, at least you're learning…And by the way, laughing at a person trying to master another language is very rude, especially if a person who is laughing has never ever tried to learn another language themselves. Never criticize what you can't do yourself. It's a very negative and cynical state of mind that can turn against you.

So, keep going! Be courageous. Claim your power. The best way to claim your power is to keep taking action. The best way to keep taking action is by combining it with attraction.

Yes, visualize whatever you want, the process and the end goal. And when you so, be mindful of whatever comes to your mind. Do you feel confident visualizing yourself in your new job or running a new business?

Chapter 2 Why Feeling More Positive Is NOT Enough

Do you feel confident visualizing yourself in your new house? Or perhaps you keep getting those negative thoughts:

I guess it's not for me, I will never get there because I didn't get higher education.

*In my country, things are tough, and the government...*and whatnot.

You need to release that. Release, let go, get rid of that. First, be mindful, allow, and accept to release. And, as I said before, don't feel guilty about having negative thoughts, it's good to dive deep into your subconscious mind so that you can eventually release whatever it is that doesn't serve you. And with that ability, you can keep moving up and designing your life exactly the way you want. You will feel confident knowing you have the tools that allow you to move to the next level. I am not saying that you will do one exercise and then everything will manifest, magically. It is a process.

You will be using this process to reach the next level, then, the next level will feel normal, and you will come across other mind limitations, and you will release them too. It's still a step-by-step journey.

Millionaires, and us, the Abundant Mindset People who are studying wealth and are on their way to reach their abundance goals, understand the power of process and trusting it.

Millionaires also experience challenges. And they also need the tools to help them get rid of their limitations in different areas of life. Problems make us stronger. Our limitations can be turned into our biggest power and asset.

So, no more victim mentality, be responsible, and it will feel so good. As someone who has made that shift, I also need to warn you, as you shift from a victim mindset to a responsible mindset, some guilt and shame may arise.

Keep releasing them. Personally, I do my releases through meditation. I just set my intention, sit still, and breathe, and then I focus on the positive!)

Chapter 2 Why Feeling More Positive Is NOT Enough

Another way to release negative emotions to move forward is EFT (Emotional Freedom Technique via Tapping on meridian points). I am not an expert in Tapping. However, I am very passionate about it, and I do practice it on myself. I have experienced some fantastic shifts with this healing modality.

(To learn more about this topic, I would recommend you read the book *The Tapping Solution* by Nick Ortner (you can also find their videos on YouTube to learn faster). What I really like about Nick's book is that I was able to get amazing results, even without reading the entire book. I just began learning and practicing what the book was teaching. Needless to say, I felt inspired to finish the book to try even more of its exercises. But, to get my first results with EFT, I didn't even have to know that much about it.)

So, once again,....positive thinking must be backed up with positive action – this is the mindset for abundance!

That action can feel good, and it will feel even better the deeper you go. But positive does not always feel good, to begin with because you are breaking your comfort zone.

There is a concept I came out with. It's called the Yoga Mindset…. It's something I realized as I got started on yoga. Our teacher would always encourage us to stretch to feel a little bit of pain, "pleasurable pain" as he would put it himself. Once again, practicing a new pose may be painful. Still, later, as you dive deeper, you make friends with your emotions and even your temporary limitations.

In our yoga classes, we are also taught the non-judgmental approach, and we are strongly advised not to compare ourselves to other people. Boom! Once again, it's a great mindset to apply, also on your journey to manifest more money and abundance.

Do you compare yourself to other people and what they have (and what you don't have?). Once again, it's a fear-based mindset. And we already agreed that love-based mindset is the best way to manifest more success, peacefully and joyfully.

So many people give up on their businesses, careers and better job opportunities because they compare themselves with other people who are more advanced.

Oh...they have this and that, and who am I to be working on my goals? I feel like a Nobody.

Whenever those thoughts arise, ask yourself, how can I transform frustration into INSPIRATION?

Perhaps you got a course or a program. Let's say it's business or marketing. Or LOA, or self-development.

Heck, maybe it's even health and fitness or weight loss. The course facilitator puts you and other course participants in a Facebook group, all with good intentions.

They believe in the power of community, and so everyone gets encouraged to share their results. Let's say you are a total beginner, just starting out. And some people in your group have more experience, or perhaps they have been through certain life situations that helped them master their mindset. They get faster results, they post them, and a lot of people get inspired. The question is- will you get inspired or frustrated?

How will you manipulate your mindset and your emotions?

As someone who used to buy a lot of online courses and programs (you should not be afraid to invest in yourself, more on that later, there is also a dark side to it, so I will dedicate another section to this interesting topic), I have witnessed all kinds of behaviors in Facebook groups related to those courses. Here's the most common pattern, someone posts their results. If it's a business course, they often post income screenshots.

So many emotions there, this topic deserves an entire book lol).

If it's a self-development, manifestation course, or anything spirituality related, they post some amazing spiritual experience they have been having.

If it's a health and fitness course, they post how this new diet helped them lose weight and before and after.

And then...the rest of the group will start messaging that person asking questions...Now, here's a million-dollar question...

Most people will ask:

So, what is your secret, what have you been doing? What is the strategy?

What are you eating?

How do you meditate?

What is your marketing strategy?

How much do you spend on ads?

If I spend this amount of money on my ads, will I also make 6 figures as you do?".

Those people are all in a trance. Unconscious trance! They have no idea what is going on.

The correct question should be:

How do you think?

What is your mindset?

And what experiences shaped it before you joined this program?

The strategy usually involves combining different tactics. For example, a person who was so successful at losing weight may be mindfully combining intermittent fasting, good fats, a ton of plant-based foods, juicing, and clean protein.

Many combinations maybe even unconscious. But a person just knows intuitively what to do, based on their mindset and different experiences that shaped them. Perhaps before joining the program, they have studied different diets and tried different things.

And they understood that there is no one size fits all diet. So they combine different healthy elements they picked form different diets. They already mastered their mindset and motivation. Being healthy is just normal to them, they need to eat healthily. Just like they need to shower and brush their teeth.

A person who teaches a massive business success, in a short amount of time, also operates from a particular mindset shaped by different experiences.

I will give you an example, which I also shared in one of my previous books (*Self-Love Handbook Amplified with the Law of Attraction*).

To illustrate my point, and show you how you can quickly shift to self-love while still maintaining a healthy touch with reality, I want to share some real-life examples, from different friends and mentees of mine.

56

Chapter 2 Why Feeling More Positive Is NOT Enough

For example, Jerry spent many years feeling depressed, which led him to drugs and alcohol. Jerry used to run a marketing company with two other business partners. The business venture sounded very lucrative and was aimed at helping small businesses with online marketing using Facebook ads and SEO (Search Engine Optimization). It was when online marketing was still new, and Jerry was very excited to be starting a company in that field.

Jerry partnered with two business associates and invested lots of his personal money into the business. He had a lot of faith in that business. He felt very positive about it, even though his wife felt skeptical and didn't like his business associates. However, Jerry had a vision of making lots of money, building a house, and starting a family. For these reasons, he decided to make a few "little sacrifices." He thought it would only be temporary, and once the business was well set up, he would be able to create an abundant lifestyle for his family.

Jerry was mostly doing sales calls and customer service. At the same time, his business associates were supposed to deliver the marketing services for his clients. Every day Jerry drove 2 hours to their office and worked there for between ten and twelve hours.

Long story short- even though the business started off very well, the business associates took advantage of Jerry's trust as soon as they could. They got involved in some illegal activities, manipulated him into signing a few documents, and disappeared, leaving him with a 100k debt.

That left, Jerry feeling devasted. Not only was he in debt, but he also felt deeply frustrated about the money and time he had invested in the business. He felt powerless and taken advantage of. That led him to drugs and alcohol. His wife left him.

Even though Jerry quickly managed to find himself a well-paid job, moved back with his parents, and started paying off the debt, he still felt haunted by the failure of his business.

He attended a few seminars, seeking answers. And BOOM, that only made it worse. One seminar was related to a wealthy mindset, and the guru told him, "Hey, you were there, you signed the documents, you invested that money, suck it up and move on! It's all your fault!"

Then, Jerry attended a spiritual LOA seminar where the guru told him, "You attract what you are, change yourself, and you will change your life, don't be so negative, you are in a very negative, victim mentality place!"

And then Jerry went to a happy motivational seminar where he was told, "Hey, just be happy, life is so amazing, just be grateful!"

All of this left him confused, and he decided not to seek help from the gurus. Instead, he decided to do some research and turned to books and videos to see what other people, who have been through hard and destructive times, had done to heal themselves.

He turned to meditation, quantum physics, and many other self-help fields. He kept going through all those materials, rejecting most of it, feeling very disappointed and let down.

Chapter 2 Why Feeling More Positive Is NOT Enough

One video he watched introduced him to the concept of self- love and the subconscious mind. That really helped him and got him onto the path of self-love.

The path of self-love helped him change his self-talk, and that led him to what I like to call "self-engineered thinking" (more on that and how you can use it too, in a second).

Today Jerry has a prosperous career as a life coach. He can now market his new business very well. In fact, he's also an expert in helping other people get more business. He has four beautiful children and a wife who supports him through the good and the bad. He also has a trustworthy team for his business. How did it happen?

It all started with a simple mindset shift that Jerry made. He kept asking himself, "What am I supposed to learn from all this? What is the path I am supposed to discover? What is my purpose? How can I transform my suffering into something meaningful?"

Chapter 2 Why Feeling More Positive Is NOT Enough

Instead of saying, "Why am I such a loser? Why am I such a moron? Why didn't I check those documents?" he switched to, "What is this situation telling me? Where am I supposed to go? Where does my new, bright future start? What do I need to do to transform?"

Every day he kept asking his subconscious mind:

-How can I love myself more? How can I forgive myself? How can I be at peace?

-How can I feel better and more empowered?

-What is the number one thing I need to change?

These are all empowering questions, and our subconscious mind is a truly fantastic tool. Please note that there aren't any specific questions you need to ask, it's all up to you. What's important here is to ask positive questions.

Instead of asking, "Why do bad things always happen to me?" or "Why do I always attract bad people?" the better questions are: "How can I attract *positive people?" and "How can I learn empowering lessons from the past?"*

Instead of saying, "Why are all the gurus the same and just want to get my money?" you ask, "How can I manifest a person, a mentor, who can really help me?"

"Where can I find a mentor who will understand me and guide me on my journey?"

"How can I attract a woman/man who loves me for who I am and not for the money I make?"

"How can I meet that person?"

So, Jerry started playing around with that. He would write his questions down or say them out loud, very often while driving, or at home while looking at the mirror. As I have already explained, these are not entitlement mindsets, these are empowering self-love mindsets.

People with self-love and self-empowering mindsets step into Courage and Patience. Those people understand that profound manifestations take time, and they are okay with that. They enjoy the process, and they feel that something unexpected is bound to happen. That deep faith and belief keep them going.

A person with a self-entitlement mindset is deep into resistance. By constantly claiming that it's all about them, that everyone is wrong and that they need everything as soon as possible, they put extra stress on resistance. Again, I have been there too, I was looking for quick fixes. I am not judging, so please interpret this paragraph as me talking to my younger self.

Your subconscious mind is like a search engine. Some research may take time. Not all the topics you search for on Google or YouTube immediately give you the answers. Sometimes you may find the piece of content or a product you were looking for on page five, while what popped up first in your research wasn't really serving you. Still, it may have given you an idea and an introduction to the topic.

So, in the case of Jerry, he started off with empowering questions and stimulated his "positive search engine." He did that while getting rid of self-guilt and "Yo, bro, just suck it up, you were there, you wired the money, you hired those scammers, you partnered up with them, it's your fault!" Jerry was able to step into self-love.

And yes, men deserve self-love too, and that is why I am writing about this case. While it's mostly women who read and research the topic of self-love, men are also invited to explore this field.

Self-love is empowering and can be used to enrich both feminine and masculine traits. I am getting off the topic a bit here, I know! Everyone deserves self-love, and it can only help us unleash the best. It works both for women and men, so if you are a man reading this, you should not feel ashamed, nor should you feel like hiding this book. You should feel proud.

Like Jerry...

So, here's how his story ended.

Chapter 2 Why Feeling More Positive Is NOT Enough

As Jerry kept asking himself those empowering questions, one day, on a pretty random drive where he was exploring a new job opportunity, one simple idea struck him. He decided he wanted to quit drinking and drugs. Most people didn't know he had an addiction problem. After all, he had a full-time job in sales. He looked all right, like a normal working human being, not some homeless drunk in the park. But every night he would drink at the bar, and on weekends he would resort to cocaine and marijuana. That was his way to ease the pain. To release the self-guilt. To stop thinking about the past.

So, after positively brainwashing himself with positive questions, he asked himself, "What if I could stop drinking? What if I could stop doing drugs?" His ego went like, "But come on. As the loser that you are, you deserve your treats. It's fun, you meet girls, you meet people. You have a good job. Soon you will be able to pay off your debt, move out of your parents' home and get your own apartment, you're good. Why not enjoy evenings and weekends?"

Chapter 2 Why Feeling More Positive Is NOT Enough

But that enlightened self-love voice went like, "But what if I could stop drinking? Would I save more money? Would I be able to take another job, pay off my debt faster, and help my parents?"

There was a bit of an internal struggle going on. One day as he was having a coffee, he saw an AA (Alcoholics Anonymous) ad, which inspired him to join the local AA meeting. Long story short, that was where he met his new wife. It was where he quit drinking and drugs. It was where he decided to take another job. It was where he got inspired to help other people and learned many valuable mindset lessons.

Today, if you ask Jerry how he got where he's at- a successful life coach with his own passion-based business- he will tell you, "I decided to become a life coach because of the inspiration I got from AA.

AA taught me a lot about mindset and self-reflection. I was able to set up a business successfully because of the extra skill I got from the second job I used to do to pay off my debt. That taught me a lot about

*work ethic and discipline and improved my sales
skills. I was able to market my business because of
the SEO and Facebook ads skills I acquired from my
failed business. Even though it was mostly my ex-
business associates' job, very often, I would stay in
the office late to follow up with clients, checking the
quality, and that led me to research. I didn't even
know I had skills that were transferable until I
started my new, passion-driven business. It turns
out that my "failed" business, hadn't really failed.*

I wasn't failing, I was practicing.

*"Oh Jerry, and how did you learn to hire people and
teach other people how to be successful?"*

*Jerry said, "Well, because of the shady business
associates who taught me a precious life lesson a few
years ago."*

"Oh, and what about your new wife, Jerry?

*Jerry replied, "We met via AA, and we shared the
same path, goal, and journey to self-healing. We
built our new selves through the power of self-love."*

Chapter 2 Why Feeling More Positive Is NOT Enough

Wow, self-love, what a life-changing concept!

Now, here's a very powerful exercise for you.

Think of one thing you are very grateful for. It can also be an event or a person. Now, go back. What happened before that? And before that? And even before that? Go back to a certain painful moment from a few years ago. The moment that is no longer painful for you. Had you known what you know now, would you have felt pain?

Allow yourself to release the feeling of self-guilt. You were not failing, you were practicing!

Stop saying, "It's my fault, I need to suck it up."

Keep saying, "What can I learn?"

"What can I do to grow stronger?"

"How can I use my pain to help other people?"

These are all very empowering questions. Remember that your brain is a search engine, so be careful what you're typing in.

Chapter 2 Why Feeling More Positive Is NOT Enough

Fair enough, sometimes life gets hard, and we don't achieve all our goals. Nobody has a perfect formula; some goals take longer. But there is always a meaning to that.

***

Chapter 2 Why Feeling More Positive Is NOT Enough

So, next time, when you compare yourself to other people, shift your mindset into:

What was their journey? How do they think? Am I willing to really turn negative into positive?

Success is a process. It's a process of ups and downs. But, here's the thing, successful people with an excellent mindset, like us, know exactly how to quickly shift out of what most people would perceive as negative. We even know how to turn negative situations into motivations, to help us generate more income and abundance...

I will show you what I mean in the next chapter. I know this chapter was a bit challenging and tough. The next one will be a little bit easier, though.

Mindset is a muscle, right? This chapter was a killer workout, the next chapter will be just as gentle stretch and a little bit of rest.

Any kind of mindset or energy work you do, give yourself some space to rest and breathe. You need time and space to internalize the new ideas and let them sink deeper into your subconscious mind so that they can successfully drive you in the right direction when the time is right.

Oh, and one more thing. Since we talked about the victim mentality and being responsible for our future...

I can hear some angry reader voices:

Elena, how can you be so judgmental! What about people born in poor countries, is it their fault? Can they just shift their mindset and become rich? It's not their fault!

Let me just tell you this- yes, I agree with you. I totally agree. I am not writing about and for those people. To help those people, I gladly donate money to relevant charities. Because when someone is hungry, it's tough to think about the mindset, starting businesses, following one's passions, etc. I think it's pretty common sense. Maslow's hierarchy needs!

Also, many LOA attraction critics point to gurus saying that everyone is responsible for what they manifest and what not. Once again, it's all about the context.

What I share and teach is aimed at people living in first world countries (or similar level) and people who have access to resources and live in safe places.

So, please don't attack me! It's up to us to make money and then use that money to help other people who are less privileged than us and need our help to live a normal life, with food, resources, and safety.

If we choose to stay poor, we can't help people in less privileged countries. Yes, you can post beautiful motivational pictures on social media, and so what. Most people who really need our help, will not see them anyway, and if they do, those quotes are not food.

Now, back to victim mentality and the mindset shift and being responsible...My personal belief is that we need to empower ourselves to do everything we can and keep taking action and work on our mindset and be 100% responsible for whatever it is we can be responsible for (our inner world and activities).

That's masculine energy. Then, we also need to surrender and let go when needed and open ourselves to the female energy of receiving. This is how an action is balanced with attraction.

Chapter 3 Why You Need to Train Your Mind to Work for You, Not Against You...

It's very easy to stay positive when things are going well. However, whenever there are some unexpected expenses, or you have to let go of some amount of money, how do you feel? Sad, angry, frustrated, and disappointed...

Perhaps you immediately "translate " the amount of money you had to spend to hours of work you had to put in to actually make it. Then you feel like you are always working for nothing, money is hard to make, and it's even harder to keep it. And once again, the negative spiral is on.

The governments and taxes. Everything is so expensive. The currency exchange and this and that.

This mindset may not seem dangerous at first. Or, at worst, it may seem neutral. Not good, not bad. Just a neutral mindset- I mean, it's healthy, we don't like unexpected expenses, right?

What if something terrible happens, what if I lose my money…these are the thoughts that accompany unexpected expenses.

But what if we could shift them into something more positive and empowering? What if we could use unexpected expenses and all kinds of obstacles to actually motivate us to take inspired action and manifest more money?

For example, last month, I had to take 2 k out of my savings to repair the roof in my kitchen. It was an unexpected expense, and at first, I caught myself thinking:

Oh no…now that I am saving some money to invest, this happens!

So, here's what I did. I allowed myself to feel negative for 2 hours. Yes. Just to spit it all out. I took a piece of paper and wrote down all those negative thoughts that I had. The most negative one was, what if I lose it all, and I become homeless?

Then, after the 2 hours of negativity were over, I mindfully decided to twist it all around. The root of my fear was that I could lose it all and become homeless!

Although the first negative thought I had was – that was the money I was saving to be able to invest.

And some of it could have been a nice holiday.

So, what I did, I took $100 and donated to a charity feeding homeless people. It felt good. And I immediately began to feel grateful for all I had. And that I had an apartment and a roof. I had the money to fix that roof.

Then, I asked my subconscious mind, what is the next step. I have no idea what to do now. Still, I have the intention to turn this unexpected repair expense into something amazing. I had no idea what to do, but I felt the energy and opened myself to all kinds of signs from the Universe.

Ok, so the last chapter, I was really in my masculine energy, and I am sure some of my ultra LOA, manifestation woo-woo people were shocked. And now, I am getting into the woo-woo energy, and I am sure the other part of my audience (money and biz people) are laughing. Once again, it's all about balance. Attraction and action. I could fill this book with some boring stuff, or I could share my own case study to inspire you.

So...I gave myself a few hours to connect with my subconscious mind through meditation. I asked for ideas and guidance. I had no idea what to do. But I felt very abundant. The fact that I have a small apartment to live in and I could fix the roof and donate to charity made me feel good.

I received some intuitive guidance to go for a walk, and then it hit me. This is what successful people (like us!) should do!

And so, I asked myself, how can I turn my unexpected expenses into motivation to earn more income? Did it happen to me, or for me?

Heck, it's not even about the roof and 2 k. What's more, empowering it's the mindset around it. The simple shift in thinking. The universe thinks you can do more and be more. So, it's testing you. It's telling you, hey, we are giving you a little challenge this month, because we know you asked for abundance. And we know that by giving you some unexpected expenses this month, you will be more proactive, and you will find different ways to increase your income.

So, I called some old prospects and generated a couple more sales in my business. Nothing unusual. But before my unexpected roof expense, I kind of procrastinated about it, and I felt very comfortable.

My mind would keep me safe:

Elena, for God's sake, don't call those people, they will say you are too salesy!

Once again, everyone is different. And everyone creates various means of earning an income, based on their skills and experience. How I manifested that 2 k back into my life, is not as important as the mindset behind it.

You don't have to do the exact same thing I did (unless you can because you have a list of prospects you can call and an offer you can make). But try to apply my mindset. Whenever faced with unexpected expenses or any expenses really, and whenever scared that you can lose it all, intend to transform challenge into an opportunity.

The Universe is showing you that you are capable of much more, and this is why you can pay those unexpected expenses. The Universe knows you can make it back (and even more) quickly.

You have probably heard some stories of millionaires who, for some reason, lost it all and still rebuilt themselves very quickly (and very often gained even more wealth). Why?

Mindset baby! They just knew the mindset that I just shared here. And yes, they also had the skills. But the exciting part is that some of them were able to re-built themselves in a completely new industry that required different skills, and thanks to their unshakable mindset, we're able to acquire those skills very fast.

I have already talked about the lottery....and how some people can manifest winning it then lose it, mismanage their money and can't repeat it. Once again, it's the mindset. An unshakable money mindset can raise your vibration and create the new energy of success, almost on autopilot. The most abundant people (and people like us who are very close!), eventually apply this mindset unconsciously.

So, next time you are paying your bills or other invoices, see them as a sign from the Universe. How can you make it back? And how can you double and triple it? Hold the intention and keep researching different ways of earning an extra income. Be confident, your subconscious mind will connect you with the right idea!

Extra Recommendation for You:

To improve your money mindset, you need to know exactly what your blocks are and how you can easily release them.

In order to do so, I highly recommend you take this free Money-Mindset-Vibration test:

www.LOAforSuccess.com/money-test

Just relax and enjoy the journey of letting go!

Chapter 4 The 5D Marketing, Spiritual Money People & How LOA Gurus Really Make Their Money and What They Don't Want You to Know

So, there is this pattern I see amongst many of my friends and readers. Just think positive, and it will be OK. And yes, I am all for LOA and positivity. I love positive stuff. And I have already shown you how you can turn negative into positive.

But, there is a dark side to it as well. Blind positivity can be negative. Positive thinking without positive action can be just some positive day-dreaming. I mean, it's OK, and it can put you in a happier mood, all good. But this is a money mindset book, so the question is, what kind of thinking can really help you create more abundance and money?

So yea, blind positive thinking can be detrimental. On the other side of the spectrum, mindful negativity can lead to joy and success. Here is how it works.

Simple example. I recently talked to a very wealthy online marketing friend of mine. Funny thing, he told me that his wealth got created from negativity. He took massive action to make money because his old situation of being broke was just too painful for him.

He kept having negative thoughts of being old, sick, and poor. Thoughts of how he would not be living to his full potential. He turned those negative thoughts into positive action, in a very simple and direct way.

He just got very upset about his situation, and that led him to study new skills. So, he studied copywriting and paid ads and search engine optimization.

And he could have said, oh, but I have a degree in languages, not in marketing. And there are no jobs, so I guess I will just wait. No! He decided to study again and got new skills that led him to abundance.

Oh, and I can hear some voices of criticism:

But Elena! Not everyone has the money to pay for advanced education! It's expensive to study marketing and business.

Well, guess what. He didn't spend that much on his education. When it comes to business or marketing, it's all about practical knowledge. While expensive University degrees are definitely required for some professions (doctors, medical professionals, lawyers, school teachers, engineers, etc.), business and marketing is more of a practical skill that can be learned from people who are in business. There is lots of free or inexpensive information available in books (can be obtained for free from the library), and online. You can learn directly from the best entrepreneurs and business experts in the world!

At the beginning stage of acquiring new skills, my friend spent hardly anything. He was studying from books and online videos. Then, as he set up his agency and began making money, yes, he paid for more expensive courses created by reputable marketing experts (not all of them had a university degree in business or marketing) to gain even more knowledge.

Oh, but he must have had plenty of free time then! Who has the time to study?

Well, he had a full-time job and a family too. But every morning, before going to work, he would put in 2 hours to learn paid ads and copywriting. At lunch break, he would read mindset and business books written by successful entrepreneurs. In the evening, after hanging out with his family and relaxing for a bit, once again, he would put in 1-2 hours of work, setting up some ads, and testing his new skills. Saturdays, he would work all day, and Sundays -off for health and family. He just stopped going out to bars with his less-ambitious colleagues. He began eating very clean and quit drinking to have more focus and energy. Then, everything aligned, and he manifested!

Never blame the lack of money or time. There is always a way. And yes, as I said, the guy's main mindset was to avoid negativity and negative circumstances by taking positive and firm action.

Yes, he also meditated and visualized and affirmed. He asked for focus, health, and energy because he knew that with more energy, he could easily work and study new skills.

Once he started generating money in his side business, he began investing some of that money into more advanced paid courses created by people with a proven track record. Eventually, he could quit his job, and he went full time with his own company and grew from there.

That's an inspiration! Positive action always beats negativity!

At the same time, I have met many people who act positive and seem positive, yet they can never manifest.

You see, you can be positive and think positive thoughts and never do anything constructive with it.

Once again, nothing wrong with that, if your only goal is manifesting happiness and balance. That's awesome too!

However, if you want to manifest money and abundance, allow yourself to back up positive thinking with positive action.

For some reason, some people choose to live in hope, too afraid to do something, too scared to take action, and even more afraid to take action from a place of curiosity.

Don't be one of them...If you ever get stuck, simply do the exercise from the first chapter of this book. Write out all the negativity and then turn it into positivity backed up by positive action.

Start asking yourself empowering questions such as:

-what new skill can I learn to get a pay rise (if you work for a company)

-who can I partner with to generate more revenue for my business?

-who can help me? Who can I reach out to?

-what can I do to have more energy to work on my side business?

-what negative thought patterns can I release today to stop procrastinating?

Real procrastination means suffering. It's when you want to do something, you know what's right for you, and for some reason, you put it off. If that ever happens to you, it means there are some subconscious blocks holding you back. Consciously you may know that taking action will make you happy, but a part of you (actually around 95% of you, as this is your subconscious mind) makes you sabotage your actions.

If, however, you just day-dream about something and never get to do it, it's not even that important to you, then it's not procrastination. For example, I used to daydream about becoming a yoga teacher. Still, I never took any action, and I don't really regret it as it wasn't my path anyway.

But, if you really want to become a yoga teacher, maybe offer your own retreats, and for some reason, you are too afraid to take action, dive deeper to check what is holding you back. Perhaps you get inspired by other yoga teachers, and you want to be like them, maybe even some healthy jealousy lurks in.

Yet, for some reason, you never take that first step. Well, you need to peel the onion of your subconscious mind. Someone around you probably said something negative about yoga, or similar line of work, maybe you were a small kid back then, and can't remember it. However, you still carry it in your subconscious mind.

I have already suggested EFT as traditional therapy. You can easily teach yourself the basics by watching YouTube videos to gradually get to the root of the problem while releasing whatever it is that no longer serves you. In some cases, you don't even need to know what it is and what caused it. Just have the intention to release it.

And, remember about our journaling exercise from the first chapters. You can totally detox from the negativity!

The real question is...

Is your subconscious mind positive, do you detox it, are you diving deep? Most of the "just think positive " stuff out there barely scratches the surface of real self-development. Yes, we can be 5% positive, and the rest of us, our subconscious mind is 95% negative. The question is. Will we get the money and abundance we desire? Diving deep is the answer!

Another question to ask yourself is:

Are you afraid of talking about money and counting money?

How do you feel about setting money goals? Once again, I am not asking you those questions to upset you. I used to hate those questions, too (when my money mindset was poor). Now I love them because they remind me how far I have come on my journey. Ask yourself how you feel about counting money, checking your bank account, and setting money goals.

If you feel anxious, keep peeling the onion. Ask your subconscious mind – why do I feel anxious?

When checking your bank account statement, check them from a place of abundance and empowerment.

Be grateful for every single dollar you see, and remind yourself that some people don't even have bank accounts. Then, even if right now you are not happy with what you see, or you would like to see more (how can you be so greedy! Haha, kidding!), start asking yourself:

How would it feel to see what I see multiplied by 10? How would it feel to make what other people make in a month, in just one day?

What would I do with more money?

Then, affirm to your subconscious mind:

It's safe for me to make more money. It's safe for me to be abundant. It's safe for me to give and share.

At the end of the day, it's all about combining masculine with feminine.

I have been around the 2 worlds...*The super masculine, hustle, entrepreneurship, marketing, and sales*. And I have also been around spirituality and law of attraction. *The feminine energy. Just manifest, stay aligned, focus on the positive. Do less and allow more.*

I love both worlds, and I combine them. It's all about balance. How do you think the law of attraction gurus and teachers make their money? Do they just think positive and wait to manifest? No, they have businesses they run. They create products that help other people. They offer programs, courses, and events. In other words- they also market and sell.

This is what so many people in the spirituality and self-development space are afraid of. They were led to believe that all they have to do is to put out value.

And yes, this is correct. All successful self-development teachers do create value. Successful businesses are all about value, long-term value.

But successful businesses also market and sell that value. They are not afraid to put a price tag on their offerings. They also focus on money. They have teams and accountants. They have a corporate structure. They think about money all day long.

They combine action with attraction.

It's OK to focus on money, just stick to your balance. Too much masculine energy, too much action, and hustle can burn you out. I know because I have been there.

At the same time, if you are too afraid to charge for your services, too afraid to ask for that pay rise, too afraid to start this side hustle, and charge for your services, you need to dive deeper. The good news is that now you understand how it works, and I genuinely believe you have the tools to heal your mindset.

Money is not evil if your intentions are pure. You can make money in a loved-based and conscious way. The world needs more positive (you already know what I mean by "positive") leaders, business owners, professionals, and experts.

This is the 5D Marketing and selling. You find the balance between the feminine and masculine. There is no specific formula for that, as everyone is different.

Some of you need to slow down, you hustle way too much. You need to slow down, and do some mindset and energy work and meditate just to re-align yourself moving forward. What are you hustling for? Are your goals really aligned with your true motivations? (I highly recommend you read my other book *Law of Attraction for Motivation* to dive deeper into your authentic motivations).

At the same time, some of you Manifestation People, you need to start taking action and get some new skills, start some activity and lose the fear of marketing and selling. I know you will be offering some amazing and life-changing stuff, so why would you be afraid to offer it to people? Even if you don't want to start your own business, let's say you just want a better and higher-paying career...well...you need to sell your skills to the company you want to work for. You need to start sending out your resumes and market yourself.

The simple formula is to find a balance between your passions, skills, and talents and what your market wants and needs so that you can be of service to others.

In exchange for that service, people will pay you. This is what businesses do. You can have a conscious and loved-based business.

Yes, some wealthy people are not ethical, they steal and lie, they manipulate, and they take advantage of other less privileged people.

But some poor people do the same, they also steal and lie.

It's not about the money or the lack of it, it's about the person and their energy. You can mindfully raise your income (and your vibration) by aligning to your higher self. Giving yourself some time to learn new things and to grow.

There is no failure. You don't fail. You succeed, or you learn. So, don't be afraid to try new things!

Oh, but what if you don't want to be a guru. Well, there are so many other ways to raise your income...

So, here's a little bonus to give you some ideas to take action and manifest more money. I have divided those ideas into different groups, based on your personality and interests.

Here are some questions to help you brainstorm:

1. Do you want to work online or offline?
2. Do you enjoy talking to people, or do you prefer more introverted activities?
3. Do you enjoy writing, speaking, or media?
4. Do you have a passion or skill you could teach to others?
5. If needed, are you willing to adapt and learn new skills?

Ideas:

1. If you have skills you can offer, for example, video editing, proofreading, copywriting, IT, design, go to freelance websites such as Upwork.com (do research online as many of those websites are available) and create a profile there. Have a look at the jobs posted and apply to them.

2. If you enjoy talking to people, consider getting a part-time job in sales - it's an excellent skill that you can later use in any career.
   By the way, one of the most successful LOA YouTubers out there used to work in sales. Honestly, when I saw his webinars, I was very impressed. He knows how to sell (this is why he is so successful), and he also creates incredible products that help people.
   Also, a job in sales can allow you to earn an extra or commission-based income.

3. If you are more introverted and don't like talking to people but enjoy writing instead, consider studying copywriting. It's a fantastic skill you can later monetize both on and

offline. To learn more about copywriting, I recommend *Love-Based Copywriting* by Michele PW (I have already mentioned her book before, it initiated my spiritual awakening).

4. If you have a skill you can teach, consider creating your own online courses or books. You can also create a YouTube channel or blog (it all depends if you are an introvert or an extrovert, I am a big fan of going in with your passions and strengths, as long as there are people you can serve with what you offer).

5. If you enjoy writing, you can become an author and write your own books, or you can also assist businesses and companies. Perhaps someone needs a writer to write some content for their website, or maybe they need an editor.

6. There are also many things you can do offline if you are creative. Have a look at your local area. Is there a service you can offer to other people? Perhaps you can be a cat or dog sitter for people who go on a holiday. Maybe you

can start your own cleaning company (yea I know, not sexy, but I see a lot of spiritual people with those businesses, and they actually see cleaning as an act of purging and cleansing and are very happy to serve their clients).

7. If you are passionate about helping people, consider becoming a coach. You can easily offer your services on or off-line, you can organize retreats and events. You can monetize your skills while helping other people!

Another practical idea is- if you work for a company, speak to your manager or a boss and tell them:

I really enjoy working here, and I would love to add more value to your company. And I am ready to learn new skills to help you even more. Any suggestions as for what I should learn to help you and your company grow?

If you are sending out new resumes, always write them after doing in-depth research on a company you want to work for. Focus on the "you and your" much more than "me and me and me and I and my graduation and my goals." Instead of talking about yourself, talk about them and to them and how you (and your skills) can help them.

Have sincere intention of helping the company you want to work for, and when applying for the job, make sure you understand their needs, values, and goals.

Final words:

Remove emotional attachment to money – give some of your money to someone just because you want to!

Remember when I mentioned donating $100 to a charity (after an unexpected expense of 2k) and that somehow aligned me with new actions and ideas?

I was sharing this story with a friend who is a bit negative. And what did she say?

Oh, yea you could do it because you had that money saved up. Otherwise, it wouldn't have worked so well.

And I told her that it's not about that 2 k or $100 donated. It's about the mindset. Let's say, I didn't have that 2 k in my savings, well, I would pay using my credit card. And let's say, I didn't have that $100 just to donate to charity generously. Once again, at this stage, for me, $100 is not something I am emotionally attached to.

It doesn't matter. It could have been $1. It's all about the energy behind it. So, let's say, I pay for the roof repairment using my credit card. Well, then I would ask my subconscious mind how I can pay it back as fast as possible because for me it's not acceptable to be in the negative.

My bank account has to be positive and growing. So, the mindset is always the same – how can I turn this unexpected expense into motivation to make more money?

Let's say I couldn't afford that $100 spent on charity, Let's say it was my money to buy the food or pay for the gas. Ok, all right. I would have given only 1 or 2$ to a homeless person.

Energy and mindset is everything. Don't ask me what I do, ask me how I think!

Be casual with money, tip people, and be happy about paying taxes. When tipping people or donating money, do whatever you can, just do it with good energy. Just feel good about it. Imagine that 100 readers of this book give $2 to a homeless person. Wow, in total, it's already $200 of collective donations.

Chapter 4 The 5D Marketing & Spiritual Money People

Money is good, money can help, money is not evil. You are a beautiful, smart, and generous human being, and I know you will use the information you found in this book for your highest good so that others can also benefit from your transformation.

Investing in yourself is also giving money. It helps remove resistance and emotional attachment to it. So, don't be afraid to learn a new skill. Remember, though, do it from a place of love and empowerment. Some people join courses on programs from a place of frustration and desperation. They think:

I am gonna pay this Guru, and they will change my life, now they are responsible for me and my life.

If something happens, they will blame the guru. And yes, in some cases, some programs do not live to their promise. Unfortunately, not everyone is passionately involved in loved-based marketing, business, and product creation. I have also made some poor investments myself. But guess what. I always used those experiences as a learning lesson. Now, when I buy a course or a program, I do it with a 100%

responsibility mindset. I pay for information, coaching, and guidance.

But I understand that it's all up to me. Nobody can change your life for you. You can learn from other people. And I encourage you to keep learning and keep investing. But you are the only one who can change yourself.

Finally, when you talk about rich people...

Include yourself in them...see yourself as rich and successful. I know you already are! Always stretch your mindset. Gotta keep growing and stretching.

I don't know if you have noticed...in my previous chapters I used the expressions like:

 -rich people and people on their way to wealth,

Or:

 -rich people like us

Once again, having money doesn't have to exclude spirituality. You can use the money to help other people, and spirituality is all about becoming a better person and helping other people.

Just Align Yourself with Being of Service

Train your subconscious mind into enjoying your life so that you are getting what you want.

Also, stop apologizing about what you earned, what you have, and want you want. For me, it was a big one, because I used to hang out with people who would judge me because of my money goals. And for some reason, for those people, the fact that I am a woman would give them even more reasons to judge me.

If you have a partner you love, you would tell everyone, wouldn't you? Would you feel ashamed?

You are rich and abundant. You love what you do and make amazing money doing it. All our friends are in the same situation.

You meet, and you talk about your projects and money, and nobody complains. Imagine how good it feels? <u>This is your reality now!</u>

I believe in you. You are a wonderful human being. I am here to support you. In case you want to get in touch with me, you will find more information on the following pages.

***

Before you go, I need your help. It will only take a few minutes of your precious time. If you enjoyed this book, could you please leave me a short review on Amazon?

Many people in our community will benefit from your review, and it may even inspire them to start practicing the deep transformative LOA techniques described in this book.

Thanks in advance!

PS. All my books are also available in audiobook format.

You will find them at:

www.loaforsuccess.com/audiobooks

A Special Offer from Elena to Help You Manifest Faster

Finally, I would like to invite you to join my private mailing list (my **VIP LOA Newsletter**). Whenever I release a new book, you will be the first one to find out. You can also stay in touch with me and ask me questions. Email is the only way because I am not on social media.

In the meantime, I will keep you entertained with a free copy of my exclusive LOA workbook that will be emailed to you when you sign up.

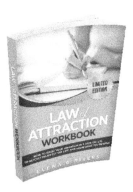

To join, visit the link below now:

www.loaforsuccess.com/newsletter

Also, remember to take a free Money-Mindset test by going to:

www.LOAforSuccess.com/money-test

Thanks to this test, you will learn more about your success blocks and how to remove them!

So, go to:

www.LOAforSuccess.com/money-test

And take your money-mindset-vibration test now!

If you have any questions about this book, please email us at: support@loaforsuccess.com

More Books written by Elena G.Rivers

Available at: www.loaforsuccess.com

Ebook – Paperback – Audiobook Editions Available Now

Law of Attraction for Amazing Relationships

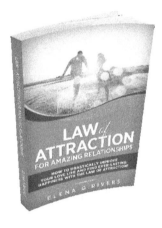

Law of Attraction for Weight Loss

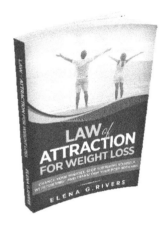

Law of Attraction for Abundance

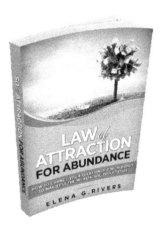

You will find more at:

www.loaforsuccess.com/books